To Walk Humbly

THE WAY OF HOLINESS

Bernard Häring, C.Ss.R.

LIGUORI CELEBRATION SERIES

D1206017

Liguori

ONE LIGUORI DRIVE
LIGUORI MO 63057-9999
314.464.2500

Imprimi Potest:
Richard Thibodeau, C.Ss.R.
Provincial, Denver Province
The Redemptorists

Imprimatur:
Most Reverend Michael J. Sheridan
Auxiliary Bishop, Archdiocese of St. Louis

ISBN 0-7648-0468-5
Library of Congress Catalog Card Number: 99-71463

Scripture quotations from the *New Revised Standard Version of the Bible,* © 1989 by the Division of Christian Educa-
tion of the National Council of the Churches of Christ in the
USA. Used with permission. All rights reserved.

Quotations from Vatican II documents taken from *Vatican
Council II, the basic sixteen documents: Constitutions,
Decrees, Declarations. A completely revised translation in
inclusive language.* Austin Flannery, OP, general editor.
© 1996 Costello Publishing Company: Northport, NY and
Dominican Publications: Dublin, Ireland. Chapter page
quotations from Bernard Häring, C.Ss.R., *The Virtues of an
Authentic Life: A Celebration of Spiritual Maturity.*
© 1997 Liguori Publications: Liguori, MO.

This is a revised edition of materials that originally appeared
in *In Pursuit of Holiness,* © 1982, Liguori Publications.

Cover design by Wendy Barnes

Table *of* Contents

Introduction

A book about holiness relates to people in different ways. Those who already have a desire to become holy—to be saints—will take time to read these pages; and my hope is that during the reading this already existing desire will increase. What a splendid reward it would be for me if, as I am dedicating my meditations, prayers, and efforts to help you find the way to Christian holiness and persevere in it to the end, I would also take a few steps forward!

But I have yet higher hopes, for I am not the only voice addressing you. Others have already planted the seed and watered the garden. God is totally interested in our quest for holiness, and will not deny any grace to those who pray for it. Here, indeed, is something for which we can truly pray in the name of Jesus; for to be holy is our supreme vocation. We believe that the Holy Spirit, promised by Christ, is the Sanctifier, the great artist who forms saints, and that this is, for you, for me, and for all people, the master plan of the Father. Christ has endorsed this master plan by his life, death, and Resurrection. I am only one voice in a great choir that sings out the invitation: "Clothe yourselves with the new self, created according to the likeness of God in true righteousness and holiness" (Ephesians 4:24).

I was privileged to be a member of the Second Vatican Council. One hot summer day, in 1963, I was working in a Council commission which drafted a text on the call of the whole Church to holiness, and an appeal to those in religious life to be witnesses and promoters of this vocation that they should see as essential for their own identity (see *Lumen Gentium*, "Dogmatic Constitution on the Church," chapter 5). At noon that day, when we left the room, we heard that Pope John XXIII was in his last agony. His entire life and his final acceptance of death had personified this universal call to holiness.

This text is at the very heart of the Council. Those who do not take it seriously enough will understand little about the teaching and guidelines of Vatican II, or, indeed, of the Bible, which is God's Word inviting us, most kindly and urgently: "You shall be holy, for I the LORD your God am holy" (Leviticus 19:2).

We are, by grace and faith, God's offspring, born to a new life in Jesus Christ. Before God, the angels and the saints, and all God's sons and daughters, our call to holiness is our noblest title. How foolish it is to refuse this noble title! If all would take this challenge to heart, and convert this Council teaching into their own and their communities' lives, we could more easily agree on most of the burning issues that seem so diverse today; the differences of opinion on myriads of minor issues would no longer divide us.

It should be clear to us that belief in this assertion makes no sense unless we make it the central concern of our hearts, minds, and wills. How to become holy is not just one question among many; it is *the most important question of our lives*. We do not aspire to be among those whom the Church canonizes as outstanding saints and models. Our hope is to enrich the life of Christ's holy Church here and now, and to persevere in being faithful to this sublime vocation and to God's sanctifying action.

One woman, who had begun to realize how vital this question is, came breathlessly one day to one who was, in his lifetime, praised by many as a saint, Saint Francis de Sales. She asked him, "How do I become holy?" His rather puzzling response was, "Would you, please, close the door more gently?"

What Francis meant by this advice resembles, I think, what a bishop said recently to an assembly of major superiors: "The first and most urgent service a bishop can offer to his diocese and a major superior to his communities is this: 'Be holy, right now!'" Be holy in all things. Let holiness saturate your whole being; let it be imprinted on your character; let it become the hallmark of your conduct.

Saint Francis de Sales had, by nature, an excitable temperament; but he made the words of the Lord—"Blessed are the meek" (Matthew 5:5a)—the cornerstone of his striving for holiness. He experienced such a transformation that he was gentle toward all creatures, and acted gently even in the way he closed doors—all out of reverence for God and people. Perhaps he discerned that this woman needed a similar theme in her striving for holiness.

All of us must constantly remind ourselves: "Be holy right now. Start, this moment, to seek holiness first!" In my case, age and illness make it particularly clear that any delay would be madness; but even if you are young and strong, nothing can justify delay. God wants you to be holy *now*. To be holy means to wholeheartedly renew your fundamental option for fidelity to God's call. You will respond with heart and mind in every area of your life: "Lord, here I am! Call me and guide me on the road to you!" Then, in time, you will make your reading of the

Bible, your participation in the liturgy, your prayerful preparation for life's decisions, all expressions of your burning desire to be holy *right now*. You will take care never to miss the next possible step that leads you in the right direction.

Bernard Häring C.Ss.R.

P.S. As you begin, it is suggested that you read—not just for a background to this book but for your whole quest for holiness—the Sermon on the Mount (Matthew 5—7) and Jesus' Farewell Discourse (John 14—17). If you do so, you can no longer doubt or forget that your call to holiness is the central message of the Bible. You will also see much more clearly what that call means.

Prayer for Holiness

God, our Father, from the beginning of our lives you call us your children, and day by day you call us to become ever more aware of your wonderful design for us: to become like you in your goodness, kindness, generosity, and wisdom. You leave no doubt that you have created and redeemed us for a life that honors our status as your children, members of the family of the redeemed.

How could we ever forget such a sublime calling? You call us, not just for some work to do, but for BEING, for becoming your masterpieces. And we exist in full truth only if we accept your master plan to make us holy, gracious, loving, and lovable people.

Lord Jesus Christ, you called Peter, Andrew, James, John, and many others to live in your company and thereby to recognize the model of a fulfilled life, the true image of the Father, the embodiment of holiness on earth. Kindly and patiently you taught them the Father's design to make them holy. In the same way, you call many millions of people—each individually by name and all of us together—to an intimate friendship with you. You came, not to make slaves but to make friends, and you invite and urge us to be your friends. There can be no hesitation on our part, for there is nothing more noble or attractive than this calling to be and to live as your friends, totally dedicated to the reign of God which you have proclaimed.

Come, Holy Spirit, enkindle my heart, my mind, my spirit, my will. Fill me with everlasting gratitude for this sublime vocation. I know quite well, from my own painful experiences, that without your grace I can make no progress on the road to holiness. I cannot even grasp fully what it means. But you are the great promise of Jesus, the great gift of the Father and the Son.

Inspire me, convert me, guide and guard me. Make me holy.

I pray not only for myself, but for all the readers of this little book. I pray for all who promote the universal call to holiness, and for all who yearn for a holy life. I pray, especially, for those unfortunate people who care more for material things than for the fulfillment of the Father's design, the Son's message, or for your promptings, O Spirit of God! I pray that all may follow this sublime call for the benefit of all humanity.

Come forth, O Holy Spirit. Make us holy, and renew the face of the earth.

Lord,
Show Us *the* Way!

*D*o not let your hearts be troubled. Believe in God,
believe also in me. In my Father's house there are
many dwelling places. If it were not so, would I have
told you that I go to prepare a place for you? And if I
go and prepare a place for you, I will come again and
will take you to myself, so that where I am, there you
may be also. And you know the way to the place where
I am going." Thomas said to him, "Lord, we do not know
where you are going. How can we know the way?" Jesus
said to him, "I am the way, and the truth, and the life.
No one comes to the Father except through me. If you
know me, you will know my Father also. From now on
you do know him and have seen him."

*Philip said to him, "Lord, show us the Father, and we
will be satisfied." Jesus said to him, "Have I been with
you all this time, Philip, and you still do not know me?
Whoever has seen me has seen the Father. How can
you say, 'Show us the Father'? Do you not believe that I
am in the Father and the Father is in me? The words that
I say to you I do not speak on my own; but the Father
who dwells in me does his works. Believe me that I am
in the Father and the Father is in me; but if you do not,
then believe me because of the works themselves."*

John 14:1-11

Jesus' farewell discourses (John 14–17) tell the enchanting story of his friendship with his disciples. He opens to them the depths of his heart and prepares them for the great event of the paschal mystery, the summit of redemption.

His words give us a wonderfully clear vision of our call to holiness as Christ's disciples, indeed as his friends and even sharers of his own life and love. He calls us to nothing less than holiness in an intimate union with himself, with his love for the Father and his love for all people.

In his farewell, Jesus promises that he will go to prepare a place for his disciples. The disciples whom Jesus called to follow him during his earthly life enjoyed his company and friendship. We too should know that he is now calling us to that same friendship, "so that where I am, there you may be also. And you know the way to the place where I am going."

Thomas, who wants to see and touch everything concretely, listens intently. He is passionately eager to know the "way" of which Jesus speaks, with all its implications. But how will *we* know the way if, like Thomas, we do not even know where we are to go? Jesus' answer is also the heart of the matter for us in our quest for holiness: "I am the way, and the truth, and the life. No one comes to the Father except through me."

Jesus, Our Way

The goal of life is God: to know the One who has called us into being by knowing us in utter love. Jesus comes from the Father; he is sent to reveal to us God's love and truth and life, and our own beginning and end. Holiness is to know God blissfully as our loving Father, the Father of our Lord and brother, Jesus Christ, and finally to see God face-to-face. Jesus, having come from the Father, returns to him through his self-offering love and Resurrection. But he does not want to return alone, or only for his own advantage. He wants to bring all of us home to his Father, as his holy people. Jesus is our *way* to God.

Jesus is not just one of the prophets; he is the "I Am" (see Exodus 3:14). Jesus is one with God in his eternal divinity, and one with God in love and glory. His humanity is taken up forever by the divine personhood of the eternal Word of the Father. Jesus knows the way to God, for the Father is always with him, one with him in the power of the Holy Spirit, in mutual, self-giving love.

Yahweh, who revealed himself to Moses under the name "I Am," assures Moses: "I will be with you" (Exodus 3:12a). In Jesus Christ, the "I Am" reveals himself fully and finally as "God-with-us," *Emmanuel.*

Father of the Prodigal Son

Yahweh has sent the Son—who, being one with God, also has the name "I Am"—to meet us where we are, in our misery and weakness. In Jesus, the Father waits for the prodigal son. Not only by word, but by his whole being and his life and death, Jesus makes known to us the Father's compassionate love for the children who left home and were lost in sinfulness and alienation. "While he was still far off, his father saw him and was filled with compassion; he ran and put his arms around him and kissed him" (Luke 15:20).

Strictly legalistic in his thinking, the older brother could not understand his father's action. He thought that his worthless sibling should be disciplined, and then be treated according to his misdeeds. The prodigal himself did not imagine that more could be granted him than the status of slave.

In this parable of the Prodigal Son, Jesus tells us plainly that when we turn to God with a sincere heart we will receive a call to return to intimate friendship, to an ongoing feast of grateful love. Wretched as we are, and unable to reach God on our own, we have no reason to despair or to doubt that we can become holy; for Jesus— the "I Am" and the "I am with you"—is running to meet us in our misery and weakness, running to embrace us and to walk with us all the way to the Father's house. His is an absolute pledge of a faithful God that we are called to holiness. Jesus tells us plainly, "I am the *way*," and he commits himself to guide us on the road. And, being on the road with us, he is already our "home" insofar as we really follow him, and turn heart, mind, and will to him.

Jesus, Our Truth

The Father, who reveals himself in Jesus and is our final home, is the *truth*. Jesus is both the Word spoken by the Father and the Word who, together with the Father, breathes forth the Spirit. Only this Spirit of truth, the gift of the Father and the Son, can inscribe in our hearts the supreme truth that God is love.

Jesus is the saving truth. In the power of the Holy Spirit, he shows us the truth of his love and his total freedom for love by giving himself up for us on the cross. By everything that he is and does, he teaches us, through the Holy Spirit, that only loving people can know the Father and the Son. Thus he becomes the saving truth for all who respond faithfully to his call.

Jesus, Our Life

In Jesus, the "I Am," is our *life*. He explains our life, and our call to holiness, through the parable of the vine and the gardener. "I am the true vine, and my Father is the vinegrower....Abide in me as I abide in you....If you abide in me, and my words abide in you, ask for whatever you wish, and it will be done for you. My Father is glorified by this, that you bear much fruit and become my disciples. As the Father has loved me, so I have loved you; abide in my love" (John 15:1,4a,7-9).

Jesus is so much our life that he shares with us his life-giving love relationship with his Father. In other words, God loves us so much as to share with us the very love in which the eternal word is spoken, and sends us the Word Incarnate. Thus Jesus reveals to us the deepest meaning of our call to holiness. He takes us by the hand, identifies himself with us, and asks us to let his own truth, the truth of infinite love, shine in us and through us.

Through Jesus to the Father

Like Philip, we have trouble understanding the full depth and beauty of the words, "I am the way, and the truth, and the life," but we are happy when, like Philip, we pray from the depths of our hearts: "Lord, show us the Father, and we will be satisfied" (John 14:8).

If we pray for good health, success, and "things" first, and only after that for holiness, we have missed the mark. We really begin to be true adorers of the one God, and are on the road to holiness, when we pray first and foremost for the purifying, liberating, and saving knowledge of the Father, for to know the Father in love leads to ever more abundance of that saving love. This prayer is all-inclusive. Then we can add prayers for health and other physical and material needs, but always in view of how these gifts may contribute to our knowledge of the Father, the True Love. In this way, we are praying that God's will be done; for God truly wants us to have plentiful redemption. "And this is eternal life, that they may know you, the only true God, and Jesus Christ whom you have sent" (John 17:3).

Praying for the supreme gift of knowing the Father is the same as praying, "Lord, make us holy." And if this is truly our prayer, the one desire of our hearts, then we know that we are praying to the Father in the name of Jesus. We are opening ourselves to the very gift that Jesus and his Father most desire to grant us. And Jesus assures us: "I will do whatever you ask in my name, so that the Father may be glorified in the Son" (John 14:13).

Loving Faith

In this same passage from John, Jesus astounds us with these words: "Very truly, I tell you, the one who believes in me will also do the works that I do and, in fact, will do greater works than these, because I am going to the Father" (John 14:12). His words speak of a loving faith by which the disciples entrust themselves wholly to him and accept him gratefully as "the way, and the truth, and the life."

Through faith, we become one with Jesus and, like him, we are open to the promptings of the Father through the Spirit. More and more, we become conformed with Jesus, who says, "the Father who dwells in me does his works" (John 14:10b).

Jesus prays to his Father for those who believe in him: "Sanctify them in the truth; your word is truth. As you have sent me into the world, so I have sent them into the world. And for their sakes I sanctify myself, so that they also may be sanctified in truth" (John 17:17-19). Consecrated in that truth which breathes love, we are sanctified; and this implies essentially a mission for the life of the world.

Sanctification, the call to holiness, is the loftiest of gifts. As such, it demands that we ourselves practice generosity. If we are holy, we are given to others and, like Jesus, we give ourselves to others. We receive and accept others as gifts of God. This creates a whole new vision of all our relationships.

Jesus answered Philip: "Whoever has seen me has seen the Father" (John 14:9b). Those who truly "see" Jesus believe in him, turn their hearts, minds, and wills to him, do everything to know him with heart and mind, and to do his work in the world: the work of love. That means they consciously allow God to do the Father's own work in them and through them, just as the Father did with Jesus.

Prayer to Discover Jesus

We thank you, Lord Jesus, Eternal Word of the Father and radiance of God's splendor, for having taken our flesh and spoken your wonderful message in human words. You made yourself the visible image of the Father. We long to see you, face-to-face, in your glory. We are grateful, therefore, for the many ways you have already allowed us to know you through the marvels of your created universe. We see the beauty of the mountains and valleys, of flowers and animals; we listen to the song of the birds and of the winds; and we study the faces of holy people; see their compassion, generosity, and purity. And all these marvels cry out to us: "Turn to the One who made all this for you, revealing the beauty of God in every word!"

Jesus, we thank you for the timely parables, stories, and symbols of the Bible, for everything that directs our attention to you. In special hours of grace, it seems your eyes rest on us, and you invite us to see you, to "hear" you. Purify our hearts, and open our eyes and our ears. For only one thing matters: to see you, to know you, and so to see and to know your Father. Lord, show us the way. Teach us to know you, who are the way, and the truth, and the life.

"Lord, show us the Father, and we will be satisfied!"

Answering
with Love

L *ove is patient; love is kind; love is not envious or boastful or arrogant or rude. It does not insist on its own way; it is not irritable or resentful; it does not rejoice in wrongdoing, but rejoices in the truth. It bears all things, believes all things, hopes all things, endures all things.*

Love never ends. But as for prophecies, they will come to an end; as for tongues, they will cease; as for knowledge, it will come to an end. For we know only in part, and we prophesy only in part; but when the complete comes, the partial will come to an end. When I was a child, I spoke like a child, I thought like a child, I reasoned like a child; when I became an adult, I put an end to childish ways. For now we see in a mirror, dimly, but then we will see face to face. Now I know only in part; then I will know fully, even as I have been fully known. And now faith, hope, and love abide, these three; and the greatest of these is love.

1 Corinthians 13:4-13

Without God's grace, we can do nothing on the level of salvation and sanctity. Our answer to God's grace is love; and that love has two dimensions. It is a redeemed and redeeming love. Only in the light of the all-encompassing love of the Redeemer and the redeemed can anyone answer the question, "How can I become holy?" And our love for God and neighbor has vigor and value only insofar as it is a response to God's own love; for human holiness is impossible except as an answer to God's sanctifying action in the grace of the Holy Spirit.

God Calls

We are called to holiness by divine grace because God's love is gracious and appealing. It is God who graces us, justifies us by grace through the gift of faith. The love that we exercise in our quest for holiness does not originate in us. It is a central truth of salvation that God *first* has loved us. We are loving and lovable only because God has created us to be sharers of the triune love and has fashioned us anew by the Holy Spirit. Sinners are transformed into saints through God loving them and implanting in them the seed of divine love.

We pride ourselves on our achievements. We boast when our names are listed in a book of *Who's Who*. But how wrong we are when we use this approach in our quest for holiness! Those who brag, "I did it! I made it! I'm a saint!" are not on the road to holiness at all.

We Respond

Holy people are grateful and gracious receivers, thoroughly aware that reconciliation, sanctification, holiness can be thought of only with thankful praise: "All this is from God" (2 Corinthians 5:18a). This awareness dispels any tendency to idleness, delay, or passivity. Those who have grasped the truth that God first has loved us, and now calls us to holiness in love by bestowing on us that holy love and sanctifying us by God's own truth, will listen to Saint Paul's words: "As we work together with him, we urge you also not to accept the grace of God in vain" (2 Corinthians 6:1).

To know Jesus and his Father is to recognize the true presence of love; the wonderful ways God has loved us from the beginning and continues to love us to the end. Thus we learn the greatest art, the art of loving God.

Saint Alphonsus wrote a kind of moral theology for everyday people who desire to become holy. He titled it *The Art of Loving Jesus Christ.* It could as well have been *How to Become Holy,* for the two meanings are the same. When the saint was an old man, almost blind, a Brother read to him from the book. Alphonsus exclaimed, "What a beautiful book!" not realizing that it was his own.

Paul's Way to Holiness

Knowing that the art of loving Jesus Christ implies joining Jesus in his love for people, Alphonsus took as basic text for his book the tender song about love in Paul's First Letter to the Corinthians. Paul calls it an "excellent way" to holiness: "I will show you a still more excellent way" (1 Corinthians 12:31).

If I speak in the tongues of mortals and of angels, but do not have love, I am a noisy gong or a clanging cymbal. And if I have prophetic powers, and understand all mysteries and all knowledge, and if I have all faith, so as to remove mountains, but do not have

*love, I am nothing. If I give away all my possessions,
and if I hand over my body so that I may boast, but do
not have love, I gain nothing.*

1 Corinthians 13:1-3

Paul did not despise these wonderful charisms. He
knew that they have their real value and meaning as gifts
of God's love, and can be received and administered truth-
fully only in that love which is the appropriate answer
to God's own love. In this song of praise, Paul paints a
vivid picture of love's real meaning. In Christ, God is
revealed as the One who *is* love; so where Paul says "love,"
we could instead say "Christ" or "the Father." Only then
can we understand the infinite dimension of that love
which is "patient...kind...not envious or boastful or arrogant or rude....does not insist on its own way...is not
irritable or resentful...does not rejoice in wrongdoing,
but rejoices in the truth....bears all things, believes all
things, hopes all things, endures all things."

Saint Augustine wrote that "the singer...is the new
song." If we have become a new creation in Christ, gladly
accepting our call to holiness, then we can not only sing
with Christ the song of redeeming love, but we can make
ourselves become a part of the song. The redeemed and
redeeming love by which we follow Christ is the most
beautiful melody in which heaven and earth, God and
the saints, delight.

Christ leads this marvelous choir in which even the
disabled take active parts. He sets the tone by his own
patience and kindness. If, in difficult situations, we listen
attentively to his clear voice and see his *patience* on the
cross, his patience with us, his *kindness* to his imperfect

disciples and even to great sinners, then our own song will blend ever more harmoniously in this great melody.

Love Is Not Envious

The voice of envy can never sing the song of holiness. If we realize that we are a new creation in Christ, and that "God's love has been poured into our hearts through the Holy Spirit that has been given to us" (Romans 5:5b), we dare not sound the sour note of envy and anger in the midst of the song of the redeemed.

Love Is Not Boastful or Rude

Christ is ever aware that all he is and all he does comes from God, and his whole life and death are a song of praise of his Father. For those who sing in the choir of Christ, the same should be true. If our love is a conscious response to God's own love, we know that God alone is the "fountain of all holiness." Therefore, we do not boast; we give God the honor and the glory.

And yet, and yet....

In the charming little book, *Prayers from the Ark,* we read of a proud rooster who, perched on his roost each morning, crows to the dawning sky, "Lord, I am your servant; but do not forget that it is I who make the sun rise!" We smile, of course, at this foolish bird, but do we not recognize him sometimes in our own desire to draw attention to ourselves instead of to God, who is working in us, and to the many people who have made our accomplishments possible?

If we are tempted to boast, to glorify ourselves, we might consider the "paradoxical intention," recommended by Viktor Frankl as a humorous yet effective antidote for taking ourselves too seriously. We simply declare aloud an exaggerated version of our hidden intention: "Now I want to crow to the world about my [brilliance, skills, generosity, piety, etc.] instead of giving God and my friends the honor!" This enlightened sense of humor quickly unmasks the temptation; and it tells the evil one, with a smile, that we now know to whom the honor belongs, and that we intend to render to God what is God's.

If we are fully conscious that our life is to be lived as part of Christ's great choir of the redeemed, then surely we will never be "rude." Seeing and hearing Christ, we shall develop a fine sensitivity about matters that are unfit in this company of singers, who in all their thoughts and actions are also a part of the "new song."

Love Does Not Insist on Its Own Way and Is Not Resentful

Selfishness is the antithesis of redemption. When we wholeheartedly answer the call to holiness in Christ, we will be alert to recognize and overcome temptations arising from our fallen human nature. If we have joined wholeheartedly in the song of love, we shall quickly discover all the disguises used by this enemy of the redeemed. One of its disguises is the constant and loud claim to personal rights, importance, even "justice." But we can easily unmask all these delusions if our eyes and hearts are ever open to the divine love that manifests itself as saving justice and mercy for all.

Love (Christ) is not resentful. Christ prays even for those who crucify him, and dies for us who so often have offended him. He has come to seek the sinner, the offender.

Love Does Not Rejoice in Wrongdoing

To keep score of wrongs taints our memory, contaminates our mind, and makes us unfit for the great song of love. Here again, the "paradoxical intention" is a useful antidote. When wrongs done to us by others keep nagging us, disturbing our peace, we can be offended and take out our frustration on everyone around us. Or we can speak to the Lord: "Jesus, how great is your reign! How great were the offenses you suffered from me and others, and how petty are these things that I am storing up in resentful memory!" We can make this thought tangible by stretching out our arms toward the vastness of God's reign, and then measuring with a tiny space between thumb and forefinger the relative size of our own complaint. Then we can pray that the Lord set us free, through the power of true love, from this hurtful habit of keeping scorecards and holding on to grudges.

Love Rejoices in the Truth

In our Redemptorist community in Rome, I had an old friend who died at the age of 91. All the members of the community gave witness that they had never heard him speak of another's faults. Never to exult over the sins of others is a tremendous achievement of love, but it is an achievement that is necessary for all who want to sing the new song of love in Christ's choir.

God's enemy must feel flattered if even Christians tend to give primary attention to what is wrong with others. This places Satan first, ahead of God in our minds and hearts. We can sing in truth to God's glory only if we always discover and acknowledge *first* whatever is right, good, and beautiful. Thus we rejoice in the truth of love, whereby we help one another ever more creatively to discover the strength and the beauty of that true love with which the Spirit fills our hearts.

Love Bears All Things

Christ bore even the horrifying reality of his cross and all the insults that went with it. He faced Judas, who betrayed him with a kiss, and assured Judas that—even then—he would receive his betrayer back as friend if Judas would have a change of heart. He turned his merciful eyes to Peter, who disowned him three times. Such love stems from the great victory of the cross, a victory that will glow forever in the risen Lord. If we are raised to new life with him, we shall realize that love is the only "right answer," even to insults and calumnies. Then we can face illness and suffering, failure and frustration, as we discover our love is true and enduring.

Love lends its beauty, strength, and depth to belief, hope, and endurance. It abides forever. Christ tells us that love is the greatest, the all-encompassing reality, the most sublime beauty, the utmost strength, the full truth and firm ground of our hope. Christ confirms our hope for a share in the everlasting feast of love.

To put love first opens a treasure chest of virtues and charisms. "Pursue love and strive for the spiritual gifts, and especially that you may prophesy," says Paul (1 Corinthians 14:1). He exalts "prophecy," a special gift that he sometimes describes as discernment. When we truly love, we recognize our real needs and fulfill them in a loving manner. Then we can say, with Saint Augustine: "Love and do what you will." Christ-like love always finds the right response. In love, we will discover the appropriate "answer," even to complex situations.

Prayer to Recognize God's Love

We praise you, God of heaven and earth, for having spoken into our world the final and perfect Word of Love. You have given us Christ to offer you, in our name, the total answer of redeeming love. Let our lives, as life in Jesus Christ, become the new song which will begin here on earth and reach its eternal climax in heaven. Instill in our hearts a great desire to know you and to know your Son. Help us to recognize your love and to know ever better how to respond, under all circumstances of time and place, to your love and grace.

Lord Jesus Christ, your love has drawn us to you. The first taste of this love arouses in us a hunger and thirst for an ever greater experience of this love, and for the art of joining in your love of the Father and of all people. Love is your being and your message. Love is your invitation. It is the mystery of your heart and the revelation of your Father's love. You are love for each other in the power of the self-giving Spirit, and in your love for us.

We praise you, Holy Spirit, and we thank you for having poured out your love into our hearts. You are given to us by the Father and the Son to fill us with redeemed and redeeming love. Forgive us for so often seeking many other things first, while giving second place to what you are and what your great gift is for us: Love. Instill in our hearts a hunger and thirst for true love and an absolute trust that, with this love, all other good things will come.

Giving Thanks

When the hour came, he took his place at the table, and the apostles with him. He said to them, "I have eagerly desired to eat this Passover with you before I suffer; for I tell you, I will not eat it until it is fulfilled in the kingdom of God." Then he took a cup, and after giving thanks he said, "Take this and divide it among yourselves; for I tell you that from now on I will not drink of the fruit of the vine until the kingdom of God comes." Then he took a loaf of bread, and when he had given thanks, he broke it and gave it to them, saying, "This is my body, which is given for you. Do this in remembrance of me." And he did the same with the cup after supper, saying, "This cup that is poured out for you is the new covenant in my blood."

Luke 22:14-20

Jewish wisdom tells us, in the Talmud, that "ingratitude is even worse than theft." Indeed, few thieves are more contemptible and ungracious than those who own many things and know thousands of "truths," but never acknowledge that they have received them from God and from the goodness and cooperation of countless people. It is hard to imagine anyone more ungracious than the one who cannot see the extreme importance of this reality: Everything comes to us as a gift from our loving Father, and each gift calls for gratitude.

If we lack gratitude and a grateful memory, we cannot share in the achievements of history, since we neither recognize past generations nor discover the splendor of the present moment. We even refuse to acknowledge the fundamental truth that our very lives are gifts for which we should be grateful. We steal the honor from God, and think we owe gratitude only to ourselves.

Eucharist: Font of a Grateful Memory

Essentially, the power of humankind to mold history depends on a healthy, grateful memory. A memory is healthy and faithful if it keeps alive all the wonderful deeds of God and the worthy heritage of past generations. It opens to us the treasures of the past, gives a sense of continuity, and clarifies our present possibilities and responsibilities. It sees one's past in the light of salvation history, of the history of all generations, with Christ as center. And it knows what to save and what to discard, thereby avoiding confusion.

As disciples of Christ, we already have a head start in this area of grateful memory. In a kind of marvelous symphony, we bring into our daily celebration of the Eucharist our life stories—the stories of our family, our community, our parish and friends, our nation and the family of nations, the blessedness of the saints, the deliverance of sinners through the mercy of God. We render thanks to God for the work that was begun, and that continues in us, for purposes of making each person a masterpiece—each one unique, but all in the image of our Redeemer and our Creator.

With a eucharistic memory, we can remember and acknowledge our past sins in a healing way. As we praise God's mercy and forgiveness, the very remembrance of our own sins heals hurt memories and moves us to mercy and generosity, making us ever more sharers in God's merciful faithfulness.

The eucharistic celebration constantly reminds us that "it is our duty and our salvation, always and everywhere," to give thanks to the Father through his Son, Jesus Christ. We can truly become holy if we remain faithful to this theme of gratitude.

Developing a Grateful Memory

One way to develop a grateful memory is to count our blessings during meditation and prayer. We further train ourselves by seeing all the events of our life in the light of salvation history, and by visualizing creation through the Word of God and in view of the incarnation and paschal mystery of the Word of God. We admire the beauty of creation and redemption. A flower can remind us of the beauty of holy people, or of all the beauty that God reveals to us. Our remembrances of disturbing events, of hurts and failures and frustrations, can be brought into remembrance of Christ's passion and death.

When the doctor told me that my throat cancer necessitated a tracheotomy and laryngectomy, there were some tears; but there was also a "dance before the Lord" for the gift of faith which helps me to "make sense" of such situations—to absorb them into my communion and thanksgiving with Christ. When the cancer became active again, after a period of uncertainty, I thought: "Now, to render thanks always and on all occasions becomes the real thing!" This song of a mute man does not flow as easily and strongly as I might wish; but when it enters into the eucharistic celebration, where Christ gives himself and shares with us the power of his Spirit, a grateful memory breaks through with grace and strength.

It is easier for some people than for others, to place their heavy crosses at the scene of the Eucharist and see clearly that these crosses are not dead relics but a living share in the cross of Christ—that cross already touched by the power of the Resurrection. The memory may need more training, so that it will always quickly recall that Eucharist, thanksgiving, is the key.

Key to a Grateful Memory

Once, when my vocal cords had already refused to sing but I did not yet dare to think it might be cancer, I lost my keys, including the key to the Jesuit house where I was a guest. I retraced my steps, insofar as I could remember them, but there was no sign of the keys. I went to bed somewhat worried, not only about the considerable nuisance of replacing all my own keys, but even more about having lost my hosts' key. But during the night I dreamed that I had found the keys and was rendering thanks to God for having found them.

When I awoke, still under the impact of the thanksgiving which ended my dream, I went to one of the avenues of the city and there, in the recess of a pillar, I picked up the keys. Really! I was happy to have them, of course, but I also wondered if the experience might have a deeper meaning. Could it mean, perhaps, that to render thanks for all that the Lord sends us and asks from us is really "the key"?

A grateful memory is even key to "the key"—to prayer itself. Mahatma Gandhi tells us that prayer is the key that closes our hearts and our homes to the powers of darkness, and opens us to the light. As long as our memory is not grateful, our prayer will be reduced to a recitation of our miseries, and we shall be in danger of looking at God from a "user's" point of view. But if gratitude is the fundamental note, we shall praise God even while we offer prayers of petition.

We praise God for being so approachable, for the invitation to come to prayer with confidence, for reassuring us that we will be given even more and better than we ask for if we pray in the name of Jesus. So we offer our prayers of petition with thanksgiving. We thank God, beforehand, for all that God truly intends to give us.

We praise and thank God when we ask forgiveness for our sins, for we are assured that, even before we ask, we are forgiven. We praise God when we express our hopes, for God is faithful to the covenant, keeping all promises that we will be given the means of attaining salvation and sanctification. We thank God for everything, especially in trying situations.

Objections Answered

In the face of difficulties, contradictions, misunderstandings, calumnies, sufferings, we may ask: "How can I thank God at such a time?" We remember Christ, who never ceased to praise the Father while accepting suffering and death. Christ transformed suffering into the most sublime test of trust in the Father and love for us sinners, in expiation for the sins of the world. In times of turmoil, we will be able to withstand evil and heal whatever can be healed only if we keep alive and activate our grateful memory. Then our energies are not dissipated and wasted by impatience and anger, and our memories are not encumbered by negative impressions.

When we bring all our reasons for gratitude into full consciousness through acts of praise and thanksgiving, our difficulties will appear small indeed. We can regain our peace of mind, and properly prepare ourselves to withstand what needs to be withstood. We learn to accept that which cannot be avoided, changed, or healed.

Our thanksgiving should continue until we "feel" that the Spirit has taken over; until we are filled with a new understanding and a yet deeper gratitude. And again, let us remember that our theme of gratitude implies that we bring all this into the Eucharist, which in turn activates a grateful memory of the paschal mystery. Our thanks are offered in union with the eucharistic Christ!

Two Further Dimensions

But our gratitude has two further dimensions. The first is that thanksgiving offered to God is inseparable from gratitude to our neighbor. Unless we are grateful to people, our thanksgiving and eucharistic celebrations are fraudulent; they are only smoke screens. The second is that our self-gratitude be fully accepted: "It is good for me *to be,* since all that I am and all my abilities are God's gifts." Then our relatives and friends will sense this basic feeling and deep conviction of ours, and they will respond in kind: "It is good that *you* are!"

When we live by the truth that all people are magnificent gifts of God, we immediately recognize many reasons to be grateful to them, and frequently tell them so. Gradually, too, we come to a new understanding of the help we give to others in their times of need. Indeed, these people do *us* a service if their real needs prompt us to make the right use of our own God-given talents.

We cannot deny that people sometimes become burdensome to us, and that misunderstandings and unjustified antagonisms cause us pain. But if we faithfully use the master key of gratitude in all situations, we gradually realize that even those who have displeased us have helped us to come closer to God, have helped us to practice a more realistic Christ-like love.

When we make thanksgiving and a grateful memory our master key, or theme, we make an impact on *all* of life—personal, social, economic, national, international. How many tottering friendships and marriages could be rescued if people would stop reviving unhealthy memories, and recall instead the *many good things* they have shared? How many political compromises would result in more justice for all if each party would remember the gracious contributions of the other? Our history books, too, should recall the good deeds and worthy contributions of other nations, especially those who have at times been in conflict with us.

Does not the whole world need to take a new look at gratitude, to make gratitude its theme for living? We owe gratitude to God, and to those countless people who, out of their own gratitude for God's gifts, have contributed to the good things we enjoy today.

Prayer to Render Thanks

We thank you, Father, for allowing us to join your beloved Son, Jesus Christ, in his sacrifice of praise. We praise you for accepting our poor acts of thanksgiving and for teaching us the amazing depth and beauty of eucharistic thanksgiving. For the knowledge that a grateful memory is the road to holiness, the key to peace and strength, we also thank you.

Send forth your Spirit to pray in us, to purify our memory and our intentions, and to lead us into a life of thanksgiving and praise. Let all our brothers and sisters discover this key, or find it again if they have lost it.

Lord Jesus, we thank you for the Eucharist, where you invite us to join you in constant praise and thanksgiving, where you assure us that we will never be forgotten, and where the Church keeps alive its memory of all that you have done for it and for all people everywhere. We thank you for reminding us, in the Eucharist, that giving thanks, always and everywhere, is the master key to salvation and holiness.

Forgive us, Lord, for so often misusing our memories, for continually burdening them with unpleasant and resentful thoughts. Thank you, not only for having forgiven us but also for gradually healing our memories, and for teaching us how to use the key of a grateful memory.

Learning *to* Trust

A nd can any of you by worrying add a single hour to your span of life? And why do you worry about clothing? Consider the lilies of the field, how they grow; they neither toil nor spin, yet I tell you, even Solomon in all his glory was not clothed like one of these. But if God so clothes the grass of the field, which is alive today and tomorrow is thrown into the oven, will he not much more clothe you—you of little faith? Therefore do not worry, saying, "What will we eat?" or "What will we drink?" or "What will we wear?" For it is the Gentiles who strive for all these things; and indeed your heavenly Father knows that you need all these things. But strive first for the kingdom of God and his righteousness, and all these things will be given to you as well.

So do not worry about tomorrow, for tomorrow will bring worries of its own. Today's trouble is enough for today.

Matthew 6:27-34

If we rely on human nature alone, we will never attain holiness. But when we remember that it is God's will that we begin—it is God who calls us—we shall never lose heart. By putting all our trust in God, and offering constant praise, in gratitude for this precious gift, we shall be able to persevere. The basis of our hope and trust is God's faithfulness.

But our problem is whether we will remain faithful unto death. We can never forget how far our own fidelity lags behind God's faithfulness to us.

The liturgical prayers of Israel are marked by this realization, and they give us the key. As praise of Yahweh's fidelity and mercy continued to develop, Israel opened itself repeatedly to the healing action of God. This is also the way of the Church. The Church knows that its achievements and its fidelity are nothing to boast of; but it recognizes—and manifests beautifully in its liturgy—that in praising God's faithfulness and mercy it experiences the power of renewal and the strength of the Spirit. The Church is consoled and encouraged by its saints, who have given a faithful response. Even great sinners have—through the liturgy—found their way back to faithfulness. This happens time and time again.

Complete Dedication Necessary

We have to frequently remind ourselves of the consoling and challenging truth that one-hundred percent dedication to our pursuit of holiness is necessary. As soon as we look for a kind of "bargain" in the service of God, we deprive ourselves of the very promises God gives to those who fully accept their call to holiness.

Years ago, I remember seeing inducements for tithing that said: "Ten percent for God, ninety percent for

yourself." I cannot easily imagine a more dangerous slo-
gan. If I tithe ten percent of my time, talent, and treasure
to God, while reserving ninety percent for myself, I am
indeed an idolater! I am making myself—by the way I
think and act—nine times more important than God!
But then, of course, the God to whom I give ten percent
is no longer the living, all-holy God.

The true meaning of Old Testament "tithing" was to
give ten percent for the cult, the priests, and the poor.
This was to remind the people that their very existence,
and the goods they possessed, were God's gifts, and were
to be used in a way that honored the giver of all good
gifts. If, *in addition to* our tithing of material things, we
then put aside ten percent of our time for the liturgy of
praise and for prayer, we *begin* to see the *true* purpose
of tithing—provided our intention is to become better
able to honor God throughout the rest of our day.

We respond faithfully to the divine promises and commandments when, with all our hearts, we desire to
become holy and seek, here and now, appropriate steps
in that direction. We honor God if we expect great things,
and God offers us the greatest: the opportunity to
become holy. God's promises are not empty words.
Behind the words stand faithfulness and *deeds*. We are
invited to see all of God's wonderful works and deeds in
light of the sacraments, which are, at the same time, sacraments of faith and sacraments of hope.

Baptism

In baptism, God justifies and sanctifies us, graces us,
and calls us to be the beloved children of God. Cyril of
Jerusalem used to tell the converts of his time that the
Father, who from heaven said to Jesus, "You are my

beloved Son," was now telling them, "You have become my children." If the Almighty One accepts us as sons and daughters together with Jesus Christ, how could God then forsake us?

Confirmation

In the sacrament of confirmation, God anoints us with the power and in the joy of the Holy Spirit; God wants us to become mature sons and daughters. No other promise is firmer than the pledge made in this sacrament. God, who has begun the work in us, will complete it if only we respond with trust and hope, and strive honestly to be faithful.

Eucharist

The Eucharist, as we have seen, is the key to that total thankfulness so necessary for holiness. More than that, it provides the presence and power of the Redeemer, the assurance that Jesus is not only present externally, but wants to continue—in us and through us—his work of redemption and sanctification for all the people of the world.

In a very special way, the Eastern eucharistic liturgy emphasizes this universal call to holiness. During the litany, the faithful respond to all petitions with this prayer for holiness and unity: "Lord, make us holy; Lord, make us one!" Christ, who has told us clearly that he wants us to be one with him and one among us all—as the vine and branches are one—teaches us that holiness is, above all, the vital expression of our oneness in him and with him.

In the same Eastern liturgy, just before Communion, the deacon warns and invites all the faithful in a loud voice: "The Holy One for the holy!" This is a frightening admonition, for who would dare to say "I am already holy"? But this call invites each communicant to carefully reflect and silently discern:"Do I sincerely intend to respond faithfully to my call to holiness?"

Each time we receive Communion,we should explicitly renew and deepen our purpose to become holy and to seek out the next possible step that brings us closer to God.

Reconciliation

If, through mortal sin, a Christian has turned away from God, and thus altered his or her own fundamental option *for* the reign of God to an option *against* God's love and holiness,that one should be reconciled through the sacrament of reconciliation before receiving Communion. There is no legalism in this regulation. It is a necessary requirement because the Lord offers us this sacrament as a way of conversion and peace. Penitents receive Communion truly reconciled, and thus can experience the further purification and sanctification provided by the Eucharist.

But the sacrament is not only for those in grave sin. It is highly recommended for all;we go to the divine Healer for strength and healing *before* mortal sin threatens to overcome us. Each reception of this sacrament is a conscious recognition that the way to full union with Christ—holiness—requires radical purification.

Confidence and Mutual Responsibility

When we understand the relevance of hope and trust in God in our quest for holiness, with God's help, we will eliminate our false hopes in material goods and our human trust in our own strength and achievements.

These reasonable earthly hopes are all right, but only if they consciously give first place to hope for growth in the love of God and an active role in the divine reign, which will lead us to full and final union with him.

It is right and necessary to hope for personal salvation and for perseverance in holiness. But this is not *true Christian hope* unless we ardently desire and work for holiness in all people. By its essence, Christian hope is in solidarity; it tends to unite us in community effort. But it is absurd to think that our hope for eternal life is truly an expression of solidarity if we are not ready to share our earthly goods with those in need. The picture Christ paints of the final judgment (see Matthew 25:31-46) reveals how much our hope for holiness, and for eternal life, depends upon how we use God's gifts for the needs of other people, especially those who cannot reward us.

In this solidarity of Christian hope, we look to the saints in heaven. Their lives encourage each one of us. Our veneration of the saints, and our prayers to them, are direct affirmations of our belief in the "communion of saints." These are authentic affirmations, however, only if we are, at the same time, affirming our solidarity with our brothers and sisters on earth.

We have said that hope and trust in God demand a certain distrust of our own strengths. Our thorough trust in God does not, however, prevent us from having a healthy trust in our own inner resources. These are gifts of God. And since this applies to everyone, we recognize the good that resides in others, and help them to discover ever more their own inner strengths. Any elements of distrust are thus healthily subordinated to our *total trust* in God.

Prayer to Obtain Confidence

Lord God, we praise you for the many signs of your faithfulness and for all you have done for us.

We praise you for the great sign of hope: the cross and death of your Son, and the glory of his Resurrection; the mission of the Holy Spirit; and the foundation of the Church that you have never abandoned despite its turmoils and weaknesses.

We thank you for the communion of saints, and for the many friends who, time and again, have encouraged us.

Lord, teach us to praise you always for your faithfulness. Grant us the grace to pray faithfully and perseveringly. Impart on us endurance and trust during life's troubles. And help us to become signs of hope and encouragement for many others.

O Mary, Mother of mercy, next to Jesus Christ the Father has given you to us poor sinners as a great sign of hope and trust. You know best the costly price your Son Jesus has paid for our salvation, and for our sublime call to become images of God's own goodness and signs of Christ's compassionate love for all. Pray for us, that we may put all our trust in Christ and ask for nothing less than to become truly holy.

Seeking *the* Will *of* God

When Christ came into the world, he said, "Sacrifices and offerings you have not desired, but a body you have prepared for me; in burnt offerings and sin offerings you have taken no pleasure. Then I said, 'See, God, I have come to do your will, O God' (in the scroll of the book it is written of me)." When he said above, "You have neither desired nor taken pleasure in sacrifices and offerings and burnt offerings and sin offerings" (these are offered according to the law), then he added, "See, I have come to do your will." He abolishes the first in order to establish the second. And it is by God's will that we have been sanctified through the offering of the body of Jesus Christ once for all.

Hebrews 10:5-10

The wealth of the present moment depends on the treasures of the past, brought to light by a grateful memory, and on the strength of our hope which determines the direction and provides the power for resolute action. But the past cannot be of profit, and hope cannot be attained, unless we remain alert to present opportunities and prepare to make use of them. This is the appeal of the apostle to the redeemed:"Be careful then how you live...making the most of the time"(Ephesians 5:15a,16a). Those who do not try to "understand what the will of the Lord is"(Ephesians 5:17b), miss the mark completely. In our day-to-day living, there is no better way to both manifest our gratitude for all the past events, and our hope for the future, than by a faithful use of the present moment. In order to cherish the present moment, with all its opportunities and even all its hardships, we must learn to seek God's will under all circumstances.

Wishful Thinking

One of the great enemies of our call to holiness is the escape into wishful thinking. This syndrome wastes as much of our spiritual energies as bitter complaints undermine them. Our vocation is to be holy here and now. Our only response should be:"Lord, here I am, call me; Lord, here I am, send me!"

People gifted and graced by grateful memories and farseeing hope have the best opportunity to discover what each present moment offers. Our expectations of the Lord, both at the end of time and at the end of life, are reasonable only if we listen to God's call at the present moment and remain alert to God's coming in the future.

The more ready we are for a grateful response, the more mindful will we be of present opportunities.

The most graced and holy among women, Mary the mother of Christ, expresses her readiness with the words, "Here am I, the servant of the Lord" (Luke 1:38b). "Here am I" is a timely theme for all who have made the fundamental option to follow the call to holiness. Each moment confirms it, and deepens its roots in our inmost being and in our life's history.

We do not *really* live in the presence of the living God, the Lord of history, if we only remember that God is in history. The presence of the living God is dynamic, active, creative. When *we* live on that level, we will be alert to God's call, attentive to the Lord's coming, and prepared to respond to the Spirit of God, faithfully and wisely, in the here and now. When our whole being cries out, "Here I am, call me!" we will be graced to discover what pleases God.

Heedful of Others' Needs

Being alert and ready for God's coming, for God's call to us, also means being ever heedful of our neighbors' needs and just expectations. We continually see examples of how our neighbors—by their temperaments, needs, and deeds—alert us to signs of God's grace and call.

If those around us are kind, friendly, and helpful, they provide an environment that invites us to render thanks to God, the source of all goodness. They remind us, through their goodness, that we are called to grow in God's own image and likeness, according to Jesus' word: "Be perfect, therefore, as your heavenly Father is perfect" (Matthew 5:48).

If those close to us are unhappy, unfriendly, or even

hostile, let us remember Jesus' word: "Be merciful, just as your Father is merciful" (Luke 6:36). Jesus calls us to show mercy now, and to help others to overcome their unhappy moods.

If someone misinterprets our good intentions and blames us unjustly, we need only recall that the Lord has forgiven us a thousand times. Can we truly imitate the One who lets his sun shine on the just and unjust?

If others—in their time of need—disrupt our plans and threaten our comfort, then we pray, "Lord, here I am," to keep us aware of how far we can—and must—allow others to impose upon us and seek our help.

If some people have the bad habit of revealing the faults of others, our readiness to "be perfect" will help us to discover hów to let these persons know that we see the good, both in them and in those whose "faults" they are reporting. Choosing what we consider the "best" tactic, we may remain silent, showing by our expression that we are not interested in their carping; or we may interrupt, and mention something "good" about the maligned ones; or we may smoothly change the subject; or perhaps we have found some other means to successfully quell gossip.

Confronting Our Own Faults

If, through of our forgetfulness of others' needs, we have to "work overtime," we must learn to be patient with ourselves—to accept the commonness of "the human condition." We can apologize quietly to those whom our forgetfulness disturbed, and work on training our memories to respond better. What matters is that we do not "waste" the present moment in useless regret, frustration, or impatience.

But when we have personally failed to respond to the present opportunity and God's grace, then let us trust that God both forgives us and calls us to ask forgiveness. And while doing so, we should not lose our peace of mind, for we need all our strength and serenity in order to better use the next moment.

I know a woman who has lost several of her children through tragic accidents. When I tried to console her, she said, "I have accepted this and do not complain; but now I must prepare myself for the next test to come." This woman truly knew the meaning of preparation for the present moment. Because she had prepared herself to live her life as it came to her, with loving attention to the needs of others, she was not tempted to yield to bitterness or self-pity. Like Job, she had a grateful memory and a no less exalted trust in God.

Many people forestall their readiness to seek the will of God, and exhaust their strength through useless regrets. These are the "if only" people; those who constantly imagine that their lives could and would be happier and more fruitful "if only" their [circumstances, spouses, children, friends, environment, etc.] were different. Many marriages break down because the spouse thinks—even says!—"If only I had married someone else." But, if such a person *had* married someone else, the cry would be the same. "If only" is an evasion of the present moment, an evasion of life.

All such faults hold us back in our quest for holiness. When we spend time complaining about the "bad times," we miss many opportunities to work for "better times." Better times can be ours only when we seek the will of God and welcome it wholeheartedly.

Prayer to Welcome the Will of God

Lord Jesus, you told us that we do not live by bread alone but by every word that comes from the mouth of God. And it was, indeed, your "bread" to do at all times the will of God. At each moment of your life, you were alert and ready to please the Father by serving the poor, healing the sick, forgiving offenders, seeking those who had gone astray. Each moment was important to you, for you saw it in the light of the great hour in which you would say your final, "Yes, Father, here am I!"

Help us to learn from you, and from your beloved mother, a like alertness and readiness. Help us to recognize your presence even in our darkest nights, and to listen to your call under all circumstances. Make us ready for the great hours of our lives, and alert for the thousand small opportunities to meet the needs of our neighbors through the best use of your gifts. Make us ever better understand that we cannot pray sincerely, "Lord, here I am; call me!" unless we are attentive and sensitive to our brothers and sisters.

Learning *to* Discern

*L*et no one deceive you with empty words, for because of these things the wrath of God comes on those who are disobedient. Therefore do not be associated with them. For once you were darkness, but now in the Lord you are light. Live as children of light—for the fruit of the light is found in all that is good and right and true. Try to find out what is pleasing to the Lord. Take no part in the unfruitful works of darkness, but instead expose them. For it is shameful even to mention what such people do secretly; but everything exposed by the light becomes visible, for everything that becomes visible is light. Therefore it says, "Sleeper, awake! Rise from the dead, and Christ will shine on you."

Be careful then how you live, not as unwise people but as wise, making the most of the time, because the days are evil. So do not be foolish, but understand what the will of the Lord is....be filled with the Spirit, as you sing psalms and hymns and spiritual songs among yourselves, singing and making melody to the Lord in your hearts, giving thanks to God the Father at all times and for everything in the name of our Lord Jesus Christ.

Ephesians 5:6-17,18b-20

Task of Discernment

Discernment only works when we have wholeheartedly decided on the right goal: to be holy, to strive always toward greater holiness, to seek in all things first the reign of God, and to allow the Holy Spirit to make us loving, discerning persons.

The chief task of discernment is to recognize love for what it truly is: Love is formed in the image of God and the model of the Holy Redeemer. We cannot become discerning persons, guided by the Spirit, until our main purpose is to be, above all, loving, selfless, generous people. If our love were already wholly transformed into Christ-like love, we would spontaneously express it in the best possible way. But since we are only on the road to holiness, we need clear and specific norms.

Internal Norms

We must, first of all, watch over our *motives*. Are we truly seeking first the reign of God? the common good? healthy relationships with our neighbors? Do we sometimes allow our self-importance, our ambition, our resentment against certain people influence our evaluation of situations and actions? Those whose first, or only, concerns are their "careers," tend to assess their actions in terms of what serves their ambitions. They may do "good," but only in view of their own advancement. Therefore, many of their good deeds and words will be counterfeit, and they may be blinded to their many opportunities to do good.

External Norms

Good motives, however, are not sufficient in themselves. We also need *external norms*. The commandments, their interpretation through the moral teaching of the Church, and the doctrine on the virtues give us norms for an appropriate articulation of love. But if we have no love, or are not enough concerned about love as Saint Paul describes it in 1 Corinthians 13, these norms will not be sufficient. Our purpose may be to serve true love under all circumstances; but when the price of love is high, the norms are often ignored.

Especially in conflict situations, we realize that we cannot make an appropriate decision without a clear scale of values. Some people give the appearance of generosity, spending time and money on others, even making many personal sacrifices. Without a clear scale of values and needs, however, these people neglect the higher and more urgent needs of others, and may even oppose the best community causes. Discerning people will never ignore spiritual values in favor of material success or progress. Discerning people will never foster or promote economic and political goals to the detriment of peace and social justice on any level.

Importance of Guidance

Discerning persons take seriously their varied responsibilities for the common good. Before they act, they carefully consider the foreseeable consequences of their intended actions and words. Lacking knowledge or experience about the consequences, they will seek advice from more experienced and knowledgeable people. Such guidance does not absolve them from personal responsibility; it should enable them to act more responsibly and with greater competence.

Distraction and superficiality are common enemies of discernment. The truly discerning take time for prayer, for quiet moments before the Lord, for daily examination of conscience, and for careful planning of specific actions. Aiding them in their discernment, as they share their progress, is their spiritual guide.

Mutual Discernment

The Spirit, working in all, through all, and for all, directs our attention to the discerning community. The principle of collegiality, on all levels of the church, expresses this striving for discerning communities. In a healthy community, important decisions are made only after a serious dialogue in which each person learns to fully appraise the contribution of the others.

Before each decision, we should vividly call to mind our grateful memory. If we doubt our intention or decision, let us ask ourselves whether we can offer it sincerely to the Lord as an expression of our gratitude, and if our conscience says, "No," we reject the intention or decision.

Saint Nicholas of Flue made this act of discernment a part of his daily prayer: "Lord, grant everything that helps me on the way to thee; Lord, take away from me everything that hinders me on the way to thee." If we made this prayer our own, we would surely look more carefully at all our words and deeds, testing whether they faithfully carry out this intention.

Frequent self-examination, in the light of the Lord's Prayer and the Beatitudes, helps us to become ever more discerning persons.

Prayer to the Holy Spirit

Come, Holy Spirit, convert us, sanctify us, guide us, enlighten us, purify our hearts and minds, so that we may be able to discern what pleases you. Free us from distraction and superficiality. Broaden our horizons, so that we may be concerned as much for the good of others as for ourselves. Help us to see the needs of others in the light of your gifts to us. Help us to watch for and discern every opportunity to become holy, and prepare us to use each one generously and wisely.

Enlighten the leaders of our church and state that they may discern well the signs of the times, seeing the many chances for growth even in the midst of alarming signs. Without you, we are but fools, tending to lead others to folly. Hence we pray with all our heart. Grant us the gifts of wisdom and prudence.

Surrendering *to* God

*T*he Lord is near. Do not worry about anything, but in everything by prayer and supplication with thanksgiving let your requests be made known to God. And the peace of God, which surpasses all understanding, will guard your hearts and your minds in Christ Jesus.

Philippians 4:5b-7

*P*eace I leave with you; my peace I give to you. I do not give to you as the world gives. Do not let your hearts be troubled, and do not let them be afraid.

John 14:27

Grace Spells Peace

Paul greets the early communities with these words: "Grace to you and peace from God our Father and the Lord Jesus Christ" (1 Corinthians 1:3; 2 Corinthians 1:2; Romans 1:7). Peace is Jesus' farewell gift before his passion, and again the greeting and abundant gift of the risen Lord. The disciples heard his greeting, "Peace be with you," and when they saw him they "rejoiced" (John 20:20). In the Bible, grace and peace, peace and joy, go hand in hand.

When God turns to us and illumines us, this is grace; and if, as graced persons, we are totally given to thanksgiving and praise, then our hearts are filled with peace and joy. We are enkindled through divine light, and we are enabled to radiate this peace and joy to those around us.

Peace Brings Serenity

For Meister Eckhart and his disciple, Blessed Henry Suso, the key word was *Gelassenheit,* and all their prayer and ascetical endeavor centered around this precious gift of God. This German word is defined and described as a profound peace of soul, from which flows serenity and a special kind of composure: a graced and confident tranquility, totally different from the calmness of the Stoic code which despised the human passions and looked more for personal serenity than to others' needs.

The peace and serenity of which we speak, following the great Dominican mystics of the thirteenth century, are the overflow of a tender and passionate love of Christ, crucified and risen for us. Flowing from this is a heightened capacity to love people *in* Christ, to rejoice in all the wonderful works of God, and to minister with special care to the troubled.

Total Surrender to God

Creative detachment is emphasized in view of the highest goal: total surrender to God. Blessed Henry Suso describes the result of this surrender as "the peace and serenity of those who have found their home in God, so that they no longer know their own self in itself, but know all things and themselves in their origin." Disciples of Christ, who have found their peace in their Master, are no longer obsessed by the thought of what they need; rather, they think of what they can renounce for the sake of Christ and neighbor. The highest level of this peace and serenity is total, trustful surrender to God, even in hours of seeming desolation.

There are few of us whose peace is not sometimes threatened, our serenity not diminished by disappointment, unjust treatment, or some other misfortune. In those moments, we can turn our minds to the tremendous disproportion between the greatness of God's love for us and the relative smallness of what disturbs us. Then we may sigh, "Lord, when shall I finally have totally entrusted myself to you and found all my peace and joy in you?"

Disciples of Christ know that they cannot train for peace and serenity by self-determined mortifications. They do not have an unhealthy liking for adversities; but when these happen, true disciples greet them as precious occasions for that creative detachment from egotism which helps them to find their center wholly in God.

Suffering Contradiction

Grace and peace do not make Christians less sensitive to offenses and misunderstandings, but these gifts do allow disciples to see everything in light of the crucified love of Christ, and in proper relationship to the reign of God.

Peace and joy set all our human energies free for seeking, discerning, and doing God's will, and especially for committing ourselves to justice and peace. As Christ's disciples, we will not be surprised if, in our striving, we meet and suffer contradiction. And knowing that authentic peace and joy are totally God's gifts, we realize we can neither preserve nor promote them without continuing to give God the credit for those same gifts. It is in this context that Saint Paul wrote:

Blessed be the God and Father of our Lord Jesus Christ, the Father of mercies and the God of all consolation, who consoles us in all our affliction, so that we may be able to console those who are in any affliction with the consolation with which we ourselves are consoled by God. For just as the sufferings of Christ are abundant for us, so also our consolation is abundant through Christ. If we are being afflicted, it is for your consolation and salvation; if we are being consoled, it is for your consolation, which you experience when you patiently endure the same sufferings that we are also suffering.

2 Corinthians 1:3-6

Our Peace Mission

As a gift from God, the peace of Christ becomes the mission of every Christian. It is a sharing in Christ's own life and peace that transforms our whole being, our whole life. "And the peace of God, which surpasses all understanding, will guard your hearts and your minds in Christ Jesus" (Philippians 4:7).

We accentuate this inner peace and joy in our lives, not by a kind of pious pride, or by lack of interest in others or in the welfare of Church and society, but rather by total dedication to God's reign in all its dimensions, especially that dimension which devotes itself to the cause of peace on earth. This makes us guard our hearts and thoughts, for we cannot share and radiate the peace and joy of Christ unless we appreciate and preserve them in heart and mind.

On the other hand, Christ's disciples do not consider their peace missions to be threats to their own inner peace. They know, of course, that peacemakers have to pay the price of peace, just as Christ did; but they receive strength from the power of the risen Lord. In their dedication, while they suffer their own Mount Calvary, they do not lose sight of the Mount of the Beatitudes and the promise of Christ. "Blessed are the peacemakers, for they will be called children of God" (Matthew 5:9).

Spreading the Peace

As far as we ourselves are concerned, we try to live with all people in peace and use only peaceful means in our mission, in accordance with the biblical injunction, "Do not be overcome by evil, but overcome evil with good" (Romans 12:21). The gospel of peace to which we are dedicated is, first of all, a challenge to uproot whatever causes unnecessary discord in our lives. In constant prayer to God, we receive the grace to accept that sharp contradiction which so often is the reaction to a total Christian life. We shall speak the truth in love, even when truth will reveal the secret thoughts of unjust and violent people. But in so doing, we will show by our words and actions, the important truth that there is hope for everyone. Nobody is a hopeless case; all can convert to the liberating truth of love and justice. But it is only when our own hearts are filled with the peace of Christ that we can appeal effectively to the hearts of others, including those who oppose us.

Even our own faults and failings—which we must continue to resist—should not jeopardize our inner peace or weaken our ability to radiate its joy; for we know that God is patient and will help us in our ongoing purification. Trust in redemption, and in the faithfulness of the merciful God, allows us to smile in spite of all our mistakes and shortcomings.

This gift, to smile despite our troubles and transgressions, shows a healthy sense of humor. It never hurts others; rather, it associates us with the weaknesses common to all people and repudiates any feelings of superiority. Thus, speaking the truth in love does not imply looking down on others. A sense of humor is a ray of sunshine arising from the hearts of people who are at peace in Christ. It can also be a source of appeasement to those whose ideas, aims, or outright injustices we sometimes have to oppose.

Prayer to Receive
the Peace of Christ

Father, we praise you because, in Christ, you chose to fill us with love and peace, to be peace-makers, and thus be accepted as your beloved children. Grant that the glory of your precious gift, so graciously bestowed on us in your beloved Son, may redound in peace and joy to the praise of your name.

Fill our hearts with your grace, so that we may proclaim the gospel of your peace in all our actions. Give us strength and wisdom to detach ourselves from all forms of slavery, from anguish, aggressiveness, and useless worries, so that we may be totally free to spread your gospel of peace and joy.

Make us strong in the face of temptation. Let us ever more experience how necessary and good it is to entrust ourselves wholly to your will. Help us to praise you at all times, especially in the hour of frustration and failure, so that we may open ourselves to your consolation, and thereby become ever more able to comfort others and to call them to the way of peace.

Embracing
the Cross

S ince we are surrounded by so great a cloud of witnesses, let us also lay aside every weight and the
sin that clings so closely, and let us run with perseverance the race that is set before us, looking to Jesus the
pioneer and perfecter of our faith, who for the sake of
the joy that was set before him endured the cross, dis-
regarding its shame, and has taken his seat at the right
hand of the throne of God.

*Consider him who endured such hostility against him-
self from sinners, so that you may not grow weary or
lose heart. In your struggle against sin you have not yet
resisted to the point of shedding your blood. And you
have forgotten the exhortation that addresses you as
children—"My child, do not regard lightly the discipline
of the Lord, or lose heart when you are punished by
him; for the Lord disciplines those whom he loves, and
chastises every child whom he accepts." Endure trials
for the sake of discipline. God is treating you as children.*

Hebrews 12:1-7a

To dream that we can receive a diploma of sanctity without first attending the school of suffering is tantamount to heresy and constitutes a great danger for salvation. Christ invites us to holiness, at the same time calling us to take up our cross and follow him. "If any want to become my followers, let them deny themselves and take up their cross daily and follow me" (Luke 9:23).

Sharing Christ's Sufferings

Christ's suffering unto death is the source of our reconciliation, salvation, and sanctification. The cross, for him and for his disciples, is the way to resurrection. When we were baptized we became children of God; by that same token we became disciples of the Crucified One.

This does not mean that we should unduly "desire" suffering, but it does mean that we cannot keep the great commandments of love and participate in saving solidarity without sharing in Christ's suffering. We meet frustrations in the inevitable struggle against our own selfishness, laziness, and pride. And we must carry our own and other's burdens which, for each of us alone, would be unbearable. Saint Paul says: "Bear one another's burdens, and in this way you will fulfill the law of Christ" (Galatians 6:2).

Facing Frustrations

Parents and other educators are warned by psychologists that they are wrong if they think that children should be spared all kinds of frustrations. Parents have no right to *cause* frustration or arbitrarily *place* frustrations in their children's way; but everyone *must* learn that no one can grow to maturity without facing life's inevitable frustrations, especially those caused by one's own selfishness. Parents, who know by their own experiences how harmful it would have been if they had been allowed to yield to all kinds of selfish desires, must also know that it is a serious mistake and a sin against charity and justice to try to fulfill their children's unreasonable desires in order to avoid frustrations.

Function of Suffering

The Letter to the Hebrews teaches the function of suffering in God's plan of salvation. "It was fitting that God, for whom and through whom all things exist, in bringing many children to glory, should make the pioneer of their salvation perfect through sufferings" (2:10). God reveals the depths of divine love through Jesus, who shares with us the same flesh and blood, "so that through death he might...free those who all their lives were held in slavery by the fear of death" (Hebrews 2:14a,15).

Because of the reign of sin, humankind was exposed to suffering and death. Jesus came "to make a sacrifice of atonement for the sins of the people" (Hebrews 2:17b), thereby transforming the meaning and purpose of suffering. Suffering and death bring Jesus closest to us; they fill us with trust in the merciful God. "For we do not have a high priest who is unable to sympathize with our weaknesses, but we have one who in every respect has been tested as we are, yet without sin" (Hebrews 4:15). Jesus himself says: "No one has greater love than this, to lay down one's life for one's friends" (John 15:13). This love reached its peak when the Son of God, made human for us, called us "friends," although it was for our sins that he suffered so cruelly.

Jesus, Our Model

About Jesus, our leader and high priest, the Letter to the Hebrews dares to say: "Although he was a Son, he learned obedience through what he suffered" (Hebrews 5:8). From beginning to end, the obedience of Christ to the will of his Father was perfect and absolute. Our human experience tells us that it is easier to say "thy will be done" when everything is going well than it is when we are faced with intense suffering. Jesus knew, through both divine wisdom and human knowledge, what it meant to surrender one's will to God. He understood this in the depth of his being when he surrendered himself totally to the Father as he was betrayed and delivered to unbelievers to be crucified like a common criminal.

For us, the learning process in the "school" of suffering has further goals: expiation for our sins, purification from our selfishness, and occasion to practice our love and trust. It also offers us extraordinary opportunities to learn compassion for others.

Motives for Acceptance

One of the strongest motives for accepting suffering, even gratefully, though not with "delight," is that it identifies us with and conforms us to Christ. It allows us to suffer with him, for the salvation of all people.

We are easily tempted to think that we already enjoy the full and serene peace of Christ when things are going well. It is when we are faced with numerous adversities, misgivings, misunderstandings, and sufferings that we begin to realize the peace of Christ within us was not as firmly grounded as we thought.

When, in the midst of a storm of troubles, Blessed Henry Suso complained, the Lord asked him kindly, "Where now is your serene peace?" Jesus taught his friend that the full depth of peace comes only when one's surrender of will to the Father has been "tested"—and not found wanting—in times of trial. When we have a burning desire for full union with God, and when we come to understand the purifying function of suffering, we will be able—always and everywhere—to give thanks for this gift.

Suffering is Not Divine Punishment

For some, suffering becomes unbearable because they look at their own and others' suffering mainly as "divine punishment." They have a servile fear of God, and this is sad because suffering cannot then have its liberating effects. Our sins do deserve punishment; they destroy our peace and joy. But if we have faith in the divine Redeemer and trust in God our Father, we realize that God's purpose is not to inflict punishment, but rather to reconcile and heal us.

Though we are sinners, we should turn to God in times of suffering with complete confidence. God wants our suffering to be a remedial step forward, toward salvation and sanctity. We should even hope that by accepting suffering we can participate in the work of redemption in Christ. Liberation from servile fear is of tremendous importance in times of illness and suffering, even from the standpoint of physical and psychic healing; but it is much more so from the standpoint of our call to holiness.

A certain priest, upon hearing that I had throat cancer, made it known that "God is punishing Father Häring" for some of the theological opinions I had expressed.

When I read his letter in a weekly publication, I felt great compassion for this priest. He, or anyone, who immediately thinks of "punishment" in the case of another's suffering, will be tortured by thoughts of divine punishment when suffering comes to him/them.

I doubt that I could have survived all the illnesses and difficulties in my life if I had looked upon them only from the perspective of punishment. Of course, we all sometimes suffer because of our own faults, but even this does not mean that God "punishes" us. Rather, we can see that God's infinite goodness offers us an opportunity to learn from the consequences of our mistakes, and even more, to accept these consequences in union with Christ, who suffered for us all.

We know from Scripture that our Creator allows illness and suffering, not to "punish" us, but to give us the opportunity to glorify God in union with Christ. Even great sinners can, through the gifts of faith and grace, come to accept their sufferings as priceless opportunities for becoming holy. I remember a priest who, decades ago, left the priesthood and lived long years in an invalid marriage. He told me of his painful experiences: Never did he find an appropriate job; his wife developed a permanent illness; his children, too, fell ill; and one of his sons became a drug addict—to mention only a few of his problems. But he concluded his litany of suffering with these words: "I should give thanks to God after all, for I am afraid that I would have continued to be a domineering and proud priest. So God, despite all my faults, has taught me to be humble and not to judge anyone else."

Prayer to Accept Suffering

Lord Jesus, how happy we are that you have loved us and will love us unto death! In union with you, we praise the Father for having sent you to take upon yourself our burden and to transform the meaning of suffering and death.

Although we have experienced our share of misery, Lord, we still fear suffering, illness, and contradiction. We do not ask that you send us no more suffering, but we pray that you preserve us from suffering that goes beyond our strength. Give us the courage to accept—as a price of our discipleship—whatever is our normal share in your sufferings.

Let your Holy Spirit come upon us so that we can understand the meaning and healing power of our suffering, and bear it patiently in union with you and out of love for our brothers and sisters.

Grant us, O Lord, wisdom and generosity so that, individually and socially, we may alleviate the suffering of others and prevent unjust suffering everywhere.

Overcoming Sin

This is the message we have heard from him and proclaim to you, that God is light and in him there is no darkness at all. If we say that we have fellowship with him while we are walking in darkness, we lie and do not do what is true; but if we walk in the light as he himself is in the light, we have fellowship with one another, and the blood of Jesus his Son cleanses us from all sin. If we say that we have no sin, we deceive ourselves, and the truth is not in us. If we confess our sins, he who is faithful and just will forgive us our sins and cleanse us from all unrighteousness. If we say that we have not sinned, we make him a liar, and his word is not in us. My little children, I am writing these things to you so that you may not sin. But if anyone does sin, we have an advocate with the Father, Jesus Christ the righteous.

1 John 1:5—2:1

All Christians would substantially agree that they are neither simply saints nor simply sinners. But for those in quest of holiness, the order in which we place the words makes a difference. Should we designate ourselves as "sinners and saints" or "saints and sinners"?

In view of God's plan of salvation, we surely must choose the wording "saints and sinners"; for God has created us as images of divine goodness. In view of our own limitations as human beings, however, we have to admit that we are sinners. Saint Thomas Aquinas says, rightly, that "man is the first cause only of sin; in all that is good, the first source is God alone."

Redemption Through Grace

All of us once lived among them in the passions of our flesh, following the desires of flesh and senses, and we were by nature children of wrath, like everyone else. But God, who is rich in mercy, out of the great love with which he loved us even when we were dead through our trespasses, made us alive together with Christ—by grace you have been saved—and raised us up with him and seated us with him in the heavenly places in Christ Jesus, so that in the ages to come he might show the immeasurable riches of his grace in kindness toward us in Christ Jesus. For by grace you have been saved through faith, and this is not your own doing; it is the gift of God—not the result of works, so that no one may boast. For we are what he has made us, created in Christ Jesus for good works, which God prepared beforehand to be our way of life.

Ephesians 2:3-10

Saint Paul, who always remembered what a dreadful sinner he was, reminds us that God justifies all of us by virtue of grace. In the process of redemption, those who are justified by grace after a sinful life know that—by God's action—they have been converted from sinners to saints. They have every reason to give praise to God for the power of God's grace and mercy. In spite of all our weakness and our natural inclination to evil, it remains basically true that we are "saints."

We Are Saints

In his letters, Paul addresses Christians as dedicated people incorporated into Christ (saints):

- "To all God's beloved in Rome, who are called to be saints" (Romans 1:7a).
- "To the church of God that is in Corinth, to those who are sanctified in Christ Jesus, called to be saints" (1 Corinthians 1:2a).
- "To the saints and faithful brothers and sisters in Christ in Colossae" (Colossians 1:2a).
- "To all the saints in Christ Jesus who are in Philippi, with the bishops and deacons" (Philippians 1:1b).
- "To the saints who are in Ephesus and are faithful in Christ Jesus" (Ephesians 1:1b).

Paul, and all great pastors and Christian educators after him, have taken special care to make us gratefully aware that the basic truth about ourselves is that we have been sanctified—not, however, in a way that allows us to boast or become self-satisfied. On the contrary, the praise of God's sanctifying action, and the sense of the nobility of being a Christian, provide the strongest motive for a holy life.

It is Paul, too, who emphasizes this fundamental truth: "You were washed, you were sanctified, you were justified in the name of the Lord Jesus Christ and in the Spirit of our God" (1 Corinthians 6:11b). Sin has no right over us. We *can* live a holy life, we *want* to live a holy life, we *must* live a holy life. "Now that you have been freed from sin and enslaved to God, the advantage you get is sanctification" (Romans 6:22a).

Further Conversion

Once we have been justified by God's grace, we must continue to use all the means provided by God and the Church for further conversion and purification. For, just as Christ summons the pilgrim Church "to that continual reformation of which she always has need" (*Unitatis Redintegratio*, "Decree on Ecumenism" 6), so all Christians in their quest for holiness must continue their striving to become more fully converted. Our basic conversion to God, and the corresponding justification and sanctification, go hand-in-hand with our fundamental option for a holy life. But then this fundamental option needs to be fully ratified, strengthened, and externalized by our actions.

Knowing that we are chosen and reconciled by God's graciousness, and sanctified by the Holy Spirit, we can accept ourselves. We can acknowledge our past sins, and thereby recognize our urgent need for further purification and constant striving for a holy life, never discouraged or lazy, never self-satisfied, but also never despairing or fainthearted.

When we concentrate on the primacy of what God

has done in us, and on what God calls us to do, this does not deny the ever-present threat of sin. Rather, it helps us to see how sinful it is to yield to the desires of the flesh. By seeing ourselves as we really stand in the sight of the divine Redeemer, we can face with a certain serenity the task of ongoing conversion.

Acceptance of Others

As we face these threatening aspects of our basic self-ishness in the light of God's action, and continue to praise God's healing mercy, we also learn to accept others with their faults and failings, and to be for them signs of God's healing action. We develop a deep reverence for *all* persons, without exception.

Saint Augustine, who never forgot what a sinner he was, warns us not to despise sinners, for some who are great sinners may one day be holier than we are. This profound reverence, this trust in God's power, will also help others to discover their own inner resources that come from God.

The knowledge that we are indeed sinners as well as saints will make us more peaceful, more ready for dialogue and for constructive action. If our main concern is the evil we see in others and in ourselves, this will only make for cynicism; it will hinder all efforts to build a healthier community and a healthier world.

Only those who believe in the universal call to holiness—and who therefore always try first to discover a basic good on which to build—will be able to offer some kind of solution to a given problem with a gentle and encouraging attitude.

Dangers to Be Avoided

If we are to face the task of ongoing purification with courage and realism, we must distinguish carefully between outright sins, and faults and failings which come from our natural inclination to evil. We need to be cautious about accepting the advice of those who try to explain everything by early childhood patterns or by external circumstances. And we need not listen to harsh judgments that ascribe everything to peoples' bad will.

We know, too, that there are limits to our willpower. We cannot, for instance, change all our negative hereditary traits at once. It often takes a long time to eliminate them. Even those who have reached a high level of holiness can still have some blind spots, or be unable to overcome an ingrained habit.

On the other hand, we do injustice to God, ourselves, and our mission to the world if we think that we cannot overcome mediocrity. If once we have come to the faith conviction that God really wants us to be holy, and we continue on the right path each day, we will make steady progress. Day by day, our conscience will become more delicate, and new horizons of goodness and generosity will emerge as we gradually discover the strength of the freedom of the children of God.

When we begin to feel the peace and joy that arise from a deep union with God, from harmony with the grace of the Holy Spirit, we also can face more courageously the demands of further purification. And while we suffer the fire of this purification, our sense of union with Christ and our joy in his friendship will stimulate us even more.

Prayer for Ongoing Conversion

We praise you, Father, for in Christ you have chosen us before the world was founded, to be holy, without blemish in your sight, and full of love. You destined us—such was your will and pleasure—to be accepted as your children through Jesus Christ, so that the glory of your gracious gift, so gratuitously bestowed on us in your Beloved, might redound to your praise. For in Christ our redemption is secured and our sins are forgiven through the shedding of his blood. Therein lies the richness of your free grace lavished upon us, imparting wisdom and insight.

O God, let your Holy Spirit come upon us so that our lives may always manifest our wonder and gratitude for what you have done for us and in us. Help us, so that everything we do may praise you for your gifts. Make us living signs and witnesses of your design to call all men and women to holiness. Open our hearts and minds so that we may be able to face, with the help of your grace, our still existing inclination to sinfulness. Inspire us to be more thoroughly converted, and to live more openly, in accord with the grace you have bestowed on us.

Help us, O Spirit of God, to discover the holiness in the people whom we meet, so that we may become better able to face the evil that exists here on earth and to combat the darkness in the world around us.

Helping
Each Other

I therefore, the prisoner in the Lord, beg you to lead a life worthy of the calling to which you have been called, with all humility and gentleness, with patience, bearing with one another in love, making every effort to maintain the unity of the Spirit in the bond of peace. There is one body and one Spirit, just as you were called to the one hope of your calling, one Lord, one faith, one baptism, one God and Father of all, who is above all and through all and in all.

But each of us was given grace according to the measure of Christ's gift....The gifts he gave were that some would be apostles, some prophets, some evangelists, some pastors and teachers, to equip the saints for the work of ministry, for building up the body of Christ, until all of us come to the unity of the faith and of the knowledge of the Son of God, to maturity, to the measure of the full stature of Christ.

Ephesians 4:1-7,11-13

In the Apostles' Creed, we *affirm* our belief in "the communion of saints." We believe that we are a part of God's household, that the saints in heaven and on earth care for us, that we belong to them and they belong to us, and that they have a burning desire to see us walking on the road to holiness. Blessed are we if this faith influences all our thinking and striving, for then we shall be a blessing for humanity. Holiness—or lack of it—is not just a private affair. It matters for the whole world.

Just as the body is one and has many members, and all the members of the body, though many, are one body, so it is with Christ....God arranged the members in the body....that there may be no dissension within the body, but the members may have the same care for one another. If one member suffers, all suffer together with it; if one member is honored, all rejoice together with it.

1 Corinthians 12:12,18b,25-26

Different Calls

To accept our call to holiness implies that we will search carefully for what might be our special place in God's household. The Church needs and expects each one of us to take on our respective roles in life. The Church is holy by divine calling and grace; but whether it radiates holiness depends on you and me and on all its members. Our mutual love and concern, our unity, are basic expressions of our belief in one holy catholic Church, in the communion of saints not only in heaven but also on earth.

The Church's purpose is to proclaim the Gospel, to provide us with the sacraments, and to show us the road to holiness. We need the Church, and we owe our allegiance to it, just as the Church owes us its cooperation. Since the Church is Christ's own foundation, our love for it and our fidelity to it are expressions of our gratitude to him.

Different Responses

That the Church has weaknesses and imperfections is no reason to refuse to love or to listen to it. Jesus chose Peter to be the head of the apostles, and loved him in spite of all his faults. John and his brother, the "sons of thunder," wanted to call down fire on the village of the Samaritans who had refused them hospitality. And, on one occasion, they coveted the most distinguished places in Christ's kingdom, which they still conceived in the pattern of earthly power. But Christ's friendship and patient teaching finally bore fruit. In the hour of trial, "the beloved disciple" did better than Peter; and on the road to the empty grave—indeed, to the Easter faith—he was outrunning Peter; but he waited at the tomb so that Peter could be the first to enter it. He gave Peter love and honor, encouraging him to run the race.

There can be conflicts among men and women in the Church on important subjects, just as there were between Peter and the community of Jerusalem (see Acts 10). Paul even opposed Peter to his face "because he stood self-condemned" (Galatians 2:11b), but this did not at all mean rebellion or a lack of respect and allegiance.

It is unreasonable to leave the Church if we think, for example, that a certain bishop has made a wrong decision. We ourselves have made false assessments many times, and have failed in many ways, but this does not permit the Church to stop loving us or to care less for us. Leaving the Church, or scorning it, implies a considerable measure of false self-confidence, and a great lack of gratitude to Christ, who loves the Church so much, and loves us too, with all our differences.

If we love the Church with Christ's love, we care especially for Christian unity; for Christ's great desire for and testament to his disciples is "that all may be one."

Veneration of the Saints

Veneration of the saints—those canonized by the Church and those known only to God and the heavenly hosts—is an important part of our praise for God's marvels. If our veneration of saints and angels is authentic, then it will not lessen, but rather will deepen and strengthen our readiness to listen to the living saints, including prophets who sow seeds of discomfort within us, and all unpretentious people.

We praise God, above all, for having given us Mary, the mother of Jesus and our mother, as model of faith and holiness. From her we learn to make of our life a magnificat, a unique song of praise to God. She teaches us that God loves the humble ones, those who gladly serve others, and she interprets the signs of history as conflicts between the humble and the arrogant. She tells us that we should have great hunger and thirst for holiness, and leads us to the foot of Jesus' cross and into the cenacle to pray with and for the Church. She is pure crystal, her beauty reflecting the marvels of God. She turns all our attention to her son, and thus to God. And since she is its most noble member, she teaches us how to love the Church, and how to fulfill the expectation that we may bring joy and honor to the Church by becoming holy.

Different Charisms

Each of the saints, past and present, manifests *particular* charisms which show us how to respond to the various needs found in different situations. The lives of the saints tell us about humble beginnings, dire conflicts, and astonishing developments. There are saints who seem to remain in hidden corners of the world, yet have enriched and continue to enrich the lives of many. There are saints who seemed to live unimpressive or unimportant lives; but when God required a great decision of them or placed a heavy burden on them, they outgrew mediocrity and emerged as heroic examples of holiness.

A thoughtful look at various saints gives us an idea of how blessed the world *might* be, how admirable the interplay of social classes and nations *could* be, if at least those who *claim* to be believers would muster all their strength and, with willing hearts, set out to follow God's grace and call. There is *no one* who is unable to add a new dimension of goodness, kindness, fidelity, and creative liberty to the history of the world.

Prayer for Mutual Holiness

Lord God, by calling us to nothing less than holiness, you reveal your great love and our bond with your family of saints. We thank you for the example and the prayers of the saints. We thank you for the holy Church that leads us to you. Open our eyes to the treasures which the Church on earth offers, and to genuine holiness even outside the visible Church. Strengthen our trust in you through a better understanding of the solidarity of salvation of all the saints in heaven and on earth. They are a pledge of your goodness to us and of your power to make us holy.

Help us to recognize, ever more clearly, the gifts you have bestowed on each of us and to make the best use of them to the benefit of the Church and of all people. Show us how we can best bear each other's burdens and thus help one another to reach the goal of our vocation to be holy.

Lord, make us holy! Make us one!